3/7/08

For David Clark of [illegible]
to whom this [illegible]
Sincerely,
[signature]

THINGS HAPPEN *Poems of Survival*

THINGS HAPPEN
Poems of Survival

EMMA LOU THAYNE

Signature Books   Salt Lake City   1991

Some of the poems have been published in the following:

Verbal Events: "Awaiting Siberian Silence," "For My Child in Pain,"
"You Heal," "One to Get Ready," and "About a Dead Friend"

Dialogue: A Journal of Mormon Thought: "Dancer and I," "Meditations on
the Heavens," and "Things Happen"

Deseret News: "Remembering Five Daughters Grown Out of Home in Utah"

Exponent II: "Last Child Going to Bed" and "Love Song at the End of Summer"

Utah Holiday: "Love Song at the End of Summer"

Desert Sun: "Cemetery of Heroes," "Traveling," and
"On the Birth of My 11th Grandson"

Network: "Christmas Vigil"

Ballet West Telethon: "Dancer and I"

As For Me and My House: "Planting Wildflowers in September at the Cabin"
and "Come to Pass"

Retirement Inns of America: "In a Fitting Place" (now "Margaret at 94
Refuses a Retirement Center")

Thrasher Research Fund: "Nurse Log"

COVER PAINTING BY GARY COLLINS; BACK COVER DRAWING BY SHAUNA COOK CLINGER;
COVER DESIGN BY JULIE EASTON

∞ Printed on acid free paper.

Composed and printed in the United States of America.

95   94   93   92   91   6   5   4   3   2   1

Library of Congress Cataloging-in-Publication Data

Thayne, Emma Lou.
     Things happen : poems of survival / Emma Lou Thayne.
        p.   cm.
     ISBN 0–941214–88–5 : $18.95
     I. Title.
PS3570.H358T48   1991   91-22680
811'.54—dc20   CIP

To the light in the clearing,
and to those who have taught me to see

*"One wants to write poetry
that is understood by one's people."*

ALICE   WALKER
In Search of Our Mothers' Gardens

Acknowledgements

For encouragement, criticism, patience, and direction, I would
like to give thanks to Maxine Kumin, William Stafford, Linda Sillitoe,
Shauna Lloyd, DeAnn Evans, Lavina Fielding Anderson, and *Verbal
Events* friends; to gentle publishers who have allowed me to be read;
to Susan Staker and Lisa Bickmore for keen editing; and to Peggy and
Parry Thomas, who give me a place to write; to people of peace who
have traveled with me; and always to my family and friends, who
expand, amuse, inspire, and love me in any of it.

Contents

III
Things Happen

I.

Come to Pass

Planting Wildflowers in September at the Cabin

Easy, say directions on the can:
Scatter, rake, or stomp in gently,
spray/sprinkle till damp, not wet.

The moist seeds, webbed in the floss
of each other's company, buried alive,
come out with my fingers
winged, Gypsy-ready for somewhere new.

Shaggy, hung with their own marsh
and mountains, they cling to my fingers,
scatter like kisses on the brown hillside.

I rake them in, say,
Live here, tantalize spring.

In winter dreams
I will return again and again,
my palms wet with you,
my nails sprouting your musky scent.

And flowers, surely flowers,
wild as Gentian and Indian Paint Brush,
will grow from my fingertips,
silky bouquets to touch across my face.

And I will rise with them
no matter where I am. ❧

Sailing at 54 with a Big Brother

Unlike the bark canoes we made and floated
past the plank culvert in the creek and followed
relentlessly, stooped and magnetized, the boat
today took hold of a wind and hollowed
out a trail across a robust sea as grey
as lead, you bounding after sail and line
and hollering instructions for my novice stay
at helm.
      It worked, that being told, the kind
of deft mandate irresistible as shock
for boat and me. And now, these three days gone,
I trim that bold connection, plug in socket,
yanking up a current I could ride on.
If by that sweet redundance I'm beguiled,
it's under breakers washing up a child. ◆

Last Child Going to Bed

FOR MEGAN

Last child
home late from the campus house you played at
being away in,
back to your startled bathroom
that has crouched these three months
empty, stunned at its gleaming drains
and surfaces,

Last child
make sudden doors slide and stand open.
Create your havoc so I can hear:
—- the hearty beat of Elton John and Isaac Stern
out of your woodwork and up from your tiles
— the murmurings of your sweat shirt, your jogbra,
your tube socks dropping on the pile like ripe apples
in an unmowed pasture
— your shower in thud and downpour
under the Sassoon shampoo falling like spring
on April stung by snow
— your silence in front of the steamy mirror
saying Bride, Bride
echoing down the hall
where your sisters also played ghost
and grew out of their pictures.

The sound of water is melody in a house.
Nothing more significant.
It is the prattle and rush of what we're about.

15

Eight of us once ran it out and used each others'.

Without your running,
those tubs and sinks may toss up their porcelain
and disappear, faces unlined by tears or laughter.

You wring out your rivers
blow your hair blonded by lemon in this afternoon's sun
take a shine to bed, your bare lips
still a trickle across my cheek.

It is midnight—no—12:28.
My pen slides into the hamper
among your sleeves and collars.

Soon they will be washed and worn
out of this house of fewer and fewer waters.

Long after I find where to sleep
the hushed taps will spill the taste of you
rushing like rain to the tang and glisten
of what is there.

Last child, take the benediction of water
and leave some running for me. ❧

Morning is my Time

Morning is my time for making love. Away, anonymous
I stalk from sleep adrift in dreams that tell
me who I am. Unprotected by the surfaces I

polish in a day, deflectors set in careful
place to fend off thoughts, unconscious as the clouds
of beauty in their conformation, I cover

with a mystic wand the impertinent intrusions so
born of joy that they would curl about my edges
and claim a hand, a cheek, a burrowing, and race me,

unprotected, home. But after sleep, when morning
catches them let down and you beside me mysterious as
what has so delivered us well kept and ringing

with the music our nights have so supplied, I wonder
how my surfaces would yield to yours, or if, in
holding, there would be surfaces at all. ❧

Margaret at 94 Refuses a Retirement Center

Vintage now, under the birthdays and loose clothing
I am more than whispering out my time.
I refuse to be lost in what I have been.

With my knees bone on bone, my legs parentheses,
My back the curve of meeting itself,
I would still be a body lighted by love.

But not to be serviced into non-being.
Who can ever be equal to ease?
Even in the push-pram halt of my walker
I would tire of no grounds to be tired.

I do not want to think of my moving
like the ghostly going of tame bears
or the dancing of empty underwear on a line.

I need to be headed toward a letter,
a canyon of green, fresh strawberries,
someone at my door, laughing, roses to cut, claim.

I want more than to be the keeper of memories
the prattle of old sentences.

God still sings in my shape though more of me
goes every day to join me later.

Now an avid forgetter, still I would stay true
to keys and passages somewhere inside me,
to the words and music to "Danny Boy,"
to my soprano that never forgets.

If I am a film on slow forward,
I would like to keep sight of myself,
not to forget hurry,
hot soup, or
kissing,
to be never not touched with news of things to come.

If I let it be, this dusk has its own light
like toenails of quartz, flesh of chamois.

At the other end of childhood
my slower time is a sigh of hearing aids,
glasses, bridges, nights stuttered with getting up.
But also of instant recall of
firelight to sit by, children to teach,
work, words, arms—his.

I just need to be seen.

I am more than habit set in marble,
the sum of more than my history, my ailments,
my following, my faces.

In this time of change—and what time is not?
even when living on carpet
I will not let my feet forget earth.

Then, when an old door shuts itself
I will leave undemolished,
me, a container of secrets, set for surprise.

Few enough times in our lives we get to wake up.
I would wake swaying, I swear, like a sapling

enough to please the sky, my skin, and me

and him
in a fitting place
acquainted with the size
of who I am. ☙

Remembering Five Daughters Grown out of Home in Utah

Lying here nights on my solitary bed
I bundle you into my mind from the snaps
I've taped to the wall.

Here come your smiles! Bare knees from the boat!

At twenty above I sink into your crowding.
A swarm of familiar embraces bed down
in the layers New England exacts for the cold.

Outside my curtainless window, husky old maples
and hickory give out your names to the wind.

Like poems read in a torrent, you elbow into
my questions: How long is a sentence? How short
a stay?

Entertain me by firelight with music
and cookies. Send me your messages flavored
by lunch.

In the center of life I wake
feeding you still grilled cheese and honey
saying, All who are glad to be here
say "I"!

And hearing I, I, I, I, I.

Will even death become part
of our ease? ઢ

About a Dead Friend

FOR   DIANE
INSPIRED   BY   MAXINE

How do I tell what it is
here in the rising of hard maple
in the iron stove? This morning
while the last tag tang of winter

eases out from under the ribs
of grayed white, I throw what's left
of me into the swack, my lady-sized
axe determined on severance.

Parts fly like lovers surprised,
new edges splintered for looking.
Thirty years dead, you come out
of your letters, dear friend, smoke

from the maple lighted and already
rising. "Tell us," your children
asked almost a year ago, "what
was she like?" And I hack

my way through distances
erected for survival,
split and shivering in the cold
center of your not being. ❧

Come to Pass

This house is one half yours, Mother.
Still.

On close terms now with death, I live
in your quarters, among your mirrors
and closets, disclosed as you were
by how I muffle my agonies
and celebrate the sunlight.

If shutters make their geography
over the lace of your curtains,
I summon your naming of things
to fit the coming dark: Gumption.
Stick-to-itiveness. Heart.
Blessedness.
Coming to pass. ❧

For My Child in Pain

I would curl you back into my womb,
monitor what we ate, drank, injected,
how we slept. I would move us back further,
past conception, call on configurations
of genes, move this one, that one
by imploring the Power I never deserved.

I would offer my maiden head,
my sight, my fingers, the sound
of my streams.

I would return myself
to facing my knees in that other womb
asking my mother's rich waters to issue me
newly permitted to bear you,
to give the unspeakable joy of the bearing,
the having, the letting go, the holding
to you.

You would be safe. And we
would be born again, free. ❧

Dancer and I

As I watch, astonished,
what I hunger for
is not what I know I cannot do.
But for this cocksure witness
to what I know some other human being can:

The summoning of summer to a song,
the color of plum to a line,
the translation to the mother tongue
of what there is in flight.

Following the dancer, the cascade of discipline and
abandon like the trill of an impossible note,
I am consumed by beauty.

It is not envy nor even desire that engages me:
All is the lifting by the tongues of bells.
Here. Now.

Toes buttocks fingers instincts
tingle with places to hold and take off from
knowing for once How. ❧

Baby Horse Birthday

How could all that birthday dreaming come true?
Of ponies munching apples fallen in the back yard,
of horses living in the play house with my dolls,
of saddles with backs, not the fence to belong to.

Tonight down in this ancient barn
my mothering multiplied. The stall contained
the earth and all its flowers.
Passion, even rapture survived my childhood.

In the guise of grown-up I ran to see
when Judy called, "She's foaled! Truffle's
fooled us all and foaled when no one saw!"

And the sun was born,
wobbling on legs her head and body
couldn't calculate or stop
so they kept staggering and searching
to decipher the air and the walls and find
a place to suck.

And Truffle, magnificently weary,
passed placenta inside out, dangling
like sopped red sheeting from under
her tail that never got wrapped.

Attending to the nudging, nuzzling,
nickering to edge the baby home, she
finally pawed a crevice in the straw,
flopped down like a stricken tent
oblivious maybe to everything

but the same music I felt in my ears
that sang those nights before a birthday,
sure my dreams would come pounding true
like hooves on wood
like fairy paeans on my innocent night. ૭

II.

The Map of the World

Tourist

TO THE USSR, JUNE 7-21

Does Russia really exist?
As Israel did
     in monumental distrust and disarray?
Or England, Lake District belly deep
     in clover, cities foundering
     in new and ugly architecture?

In the Union of Soviet Socialist Republics
will there be chickens to open their beaks
and run, as in New Hampshire today?

Will there be tables, pitchers, the likes
of bougainvillaea? Acacia? Or lilacs?
The beautiful, the young, the not so, laughing?
Mamas and papas waving past our train?

How can I conjure up a tracing
of the faces, the legends exploded
or unfolding?
Like something that will never happen.

And so I write: Wait. Not the word,
but the thing hardest for me.

I want to hold onto the idea of Russia's
equivalent of bougainvillaea or acacia or lilacs.
Till I actually am there.

Glutton, I crave knowing those others,
their porches and rocks, their
neighborhoods and the details of their windows.

Do they believe in natural childbirth?
In confession? In identifying
bird calls? Is there a ferris wheel
in Moscow? A pair of hip boots waiting to wade
a stream from Lake Baikal?

Is there a hurt like pleasure
when the right word says how spring
has come delicate and sounding like a flute
maybe out there in where they say
our train will take us
in the vivid light of June? ❧

Legend: The Map of the World

Two nights ago exactly
(12 hours later here)
at the kitchen table on
St. Mary's Drive in Salt Lake City, Utah
I got out the globe and
circled half of it, went up and over
the North Pole even, to show the flight
our tour would take: L.A.,
Helsinki, Moscow.

How could we conceive of the map
I was making? Even those,
my grown children, full of more
traveling said, "Mother,
it's scary."

My halting bravado trite: "So
is the ocean, but isn't it
there to be crossed?"

I depended on maps, the globe
to assure me that places
existed. Without me.

Didn't four-year-old granddaughter Katie and I
only the day before yesterday put
together the United States of America
state by state?—Kentucky missing since
two-year-old Coulson chewed it
while we ran to catch him.

And didn't we all at the table
span the Soviet Union, thumb
to baby finger twice and a half
to take in the 6,000 miles I'll actually
go from Moscow to Siberia
and back?

Me in Siberia?
Day after tomorrow maybe.

Dostoevsky and I
remembering clean linen,
his in St. Petersburg, mine here
in Moscow. And somewhere the Kremlin
outside in the dark. &

Journal Impressions:

MOSCOW, 7-8:00 A.M., 6/10/84

1. The Burghers

Like the burghers of Rodin,
not sluggish, not taut
but at a tempo undistracted by
option
like the hidden bones of a plump face
working the faces faces faces
tucked into shoulders packed proud
of humility
dogged as despair
queuing up for fat slabs
of ripe meat
or a turn at Lenin's remains.

Disheveled like the stucco of your city,
patient as statues
do you walk alongside me
like me trying to
make sure who you are?

2. Exchange

I file my nails listening to
one last sigh of this city
evanescent as a dream.

Dollars to rubles and kopeks.

I haven't a notion the exchange.

Only that in my trimmed-down-for-travel wallet
small papers
will keep me alive.

I will go on for nearly 20 more days
breathing the strong fumes
of places not my own
drawn in
replacing myself.

Among strangers
not one of whom
knows—or cares?—
one thing about
how I breathe
at home.

3. Packed and Ready

One last look: The Kremlin east
as it should be
20 towers over the red fluted wall
the green puffs of the park
the lead patch of river
the oxidized rounds of the roofs
rusty red brick
yellow stucco
not a window irregular
cupolas strung like stiff beads
on only one
sandstone high
as at Lake Powell
looking from the boat
a million miles
to the sky. ❧

Interlude on the
Trans-Siberian Railway

"The Trans-Siberian Railway is the longest in the world."
—Fodor's Soviet Union 1984

Four thousand miles between Moscow
and Irkutsk, five days and Siberia
in between.

    Fifty years ago
that electric train in Uncle Willard's basement—
this was it
and I was on it, plunging into
tunnels, across midget cardboard farms
villages, through stations,
trestles, rivers, mountains, belonging to
the engine, choosing,
threading,
making grades: "I-think-I-can, I-think-I-
can."

    Now more than
electric or pretend, this ride just ending:
a world unto itself, this machine,
inside it me,
integral, assimilated,
its breathing, mine.

On a curve two days into
Siberia, a wide one, I leaned from
the door open between cars, strained
to see our shape, find our slant, the red
engine nosing out the track, me a propeller
urrrrrrrring on a turn: gravity, convection,
pull, centrifugal force, elemental that me.

Three days out, surprised,
as at the green like Montana in July,
a congenial Jonah, I was
contained
graded
impelled
even asleep, never still
in on digestion
circulation
eyes
sounds
momentum not my own.

Gradually I gave up
the need for maps
roads
self-propulsion.

I became the power
lines against the sky connecting forces,
a present with no past or future
scraggly dirt roads starting,
ending in themselves.

By the last, the fifth day
in our cindered, no-shower, genial sloth
I had become my favorite toy from Moscow:
a nest doll bulging red and yellow alive
inside itself seven times:

my outside—the sky, the countryside;
 inside it—the train, our car;
  inside it, our compartment, people;
   inside it, my berth above, distance,
           aloneness;
    inside it, a book, a journal, a prayer;
    inside it, inside of my head,
           inside of my body;
     last, the tiniest, far inside, God,
           the Holy Ghost
           there
telling me how to reverence being
           inside at all.
Knowing for sure why the passing of a train
could turn bottle caps into coins. ɞ

Currency

Everything was new to me.
I felt younger than the whole world.
Here was one more chance I hadn't used up.

I didn't speak the language; the only book
I could read was by me. I had to fall back on
believing in what was exalted by
the moment: a look, the sun not in its place,
the tilt of it on a shoulder, flowers, hands,

its glint at nearly midnight
behind lovers at a rail ravenous, universal,
oblivious to the laughter of the crew,
our smiles for a Saturday night and
a boat ride, on a river full of music
ten thousand miles from boats and sun and lovers
ravenous at home.

In heavy array, city streets jammed with feet;
then the Urals, the Steppe, Siberia
unjammed by anything apparent,
like a continent beyond the known world.

Across nine rumbling time zones
the curtain opening for me to experience
your daily business, you Russian:

You with the beard in the bread shop showing me
how to count. You in your high heels
in the House of Friendship counting on me for telling
the secrets of children I had to grow up to understand.

You of the burly shoulders pulling rubles from your
sagging pockets to buy a jacket American
for your vastly pregnant wife. You in the Memorial,
erasing my tears; you in the churchyard, shy madonna
with belonging to offer. You other in the graveyard
offering luck in a coin to flip
if the world won't take me in.

You in the beriozka claiming me with a peace badge,
the two of us companionable as gardens and porches.
You retrieving my lost book, me lost
on a street where anything could happen,
me measuring my frailty against
your eyeing what I didn't have.

All but one of you freeing me from the fears
that populate distance.
That one in the thick of it, given to authority,
ominous and peering still, my knuckles white with
punching buttons to close the elevator doors
on my disappearing.

Now the gift I give myself is to know
that everything in me is new,
unthreatening to you
as you are to me, each of us blameless
for not knowing sooner.

Here you are whirling inside me, you
and your rivers, your used up churches,
your waiting lines, your collectives,
your names, surnames unpronounceable as
a benediction on this holy time.

But the naming is unimportant.

It was human beings being human beings,
attending to each other.
I see in one brief lightning flash behind my grey eyes
what I owe to every one of you:

If I did all I could to repay
I would claim no currency
but my own hand
full of yours. ❧

Awaiting Siberian Silence

*"I must get back to my lovely Siberia," says my friend Valentina
on the last of her 84 days in Utah.*

The silence we both have missed like snow.
The silence that kneels inside us begging
For unfettered attention, deep and slow
To whisper from under the clutter, Get
Ready, the house that seems so full
Is merely the window waiting to rise.

It is morning. The east listens, purple,
Still. Its crimson awaits your return. Your sighs
Will be spoken in time zones fifteen away
Saying, as I will, I have been learning
How to arrive on time, late but not late.
Now I will search the plethora of firsts.
It will take silence to subdue the rush,
Siberia to grant your holy hush. ❧

Woman of Another World,
I am with You

*For women from Botswana, The Netherlands, New Zealand,
Thailand, and Russia, talking peace*

You, woman of different tongue,
awaken me.

Speak in the language of light
that flutters between us.
Open my heart to your dailiness;
give voice to your fears and celebrations
as you wonder at mine.

Your family becomes me,
the substance of what you believe
colors my view.
You take me on.

Here, here is my hand.
Filled with yours
it pulses with new hope
and a fierce longing
to let the light that guides us both
tell me where to be. ❧

In the Cemetery of Heroes

THE MORNING AFTER BUCHAREST

Under the blanket of white marble
You lie in your cradle,
A white marble cross your head board,
Your picture embedded there
As it is in my grey head.

Twenty-one. 1968 to 1989 your years.
December revolt your gift. Of the thousand killed,
More than a hundred of you here
In what just half a year ago was a park.
Above the stiff shoulders of your uniform
Your Adam's apple—a man's—
Belies the surprised eyes of a boy
Bareheaded and trying to smile—
As if to assure your mother
That yes, you are grown up enough
To be forever able and safe.

She takes a wet cloth to the white edges
Of what is left, sponges away the new dirt
From this end to that of your marble grave.
In the broken, stiff sorrow too deep
To let loose, she bends in her slim gentility
To pull the old carnations as stiff as she is,
Lays them like candles in her left hand
As she moves like a reaper around where you are.

Already planted, the edging of something
Like primroses fills the spaces the carnations
Might have left, fresh, pink-red in green.

I walk by, compelled to touch her shoulder.
She rises to meet my eyes, her hair a stylish halo
Of black and grey, eloquent as her silence.
In the language of women
I press my hand to my breast.
"Parlez-vous francais?" she asks.

"Un peu—I am American."
We look together at the marble cradle,
The dates, the boy. "A student," she says.
I feel my grandson Nicky's arms about me,
His man's voice at sixteen kidding,
"Don't let anything get you, Gramma,
"We need to water-ski."
The woman's son is mine.
I nod, point to the picture,
Say, gesture, "For all of us."
She knows.
My husband over there signals
The bus is waiting.
We clasp hands, the woman and I,
Our tears from springs deeper than any Danube.
And I know why I came to Bucharest. ❧

On the Birth of My 11th Grandson As American Troops Amass 8,000 Miles Away

Edward McKinley Heath, the doctor lays you on
    the draining belly of your mother
Wearied to scarcely smiling on her brutal bed.

Your robust father and I follow the nurse to your first
    cradle,
Watch the sponge, the stethoscope, the weights and
    measures.

In the ancient claim of rocking, I curl you into my
    practiced arms.
Light as butterfly wings, your hands
    flail the intrusive air.
The tart scent of your newborn head
    rushes a knowing through me
    of where you've been—
    and where I cannot let you go.

Six pounds, thirteen ounces is the nothing weight
    we all have passed through.
The joyful lightness of you I embrace in my soul
    like smoke rising from a chimney at the cabin
    or a phrase of music from your mother's violin.

You are the whisper of a night without wind,
    the comfort of an invisible map to follow.
How do I manage anything so unheavy?
    untrifling?

You now are the earth's creature,
>> soon to be laden with instructions to grow by:
>> this waking up—to this day, milk, then shoes,
>> new rooms, a summoning to school,
>> packs, suitcases, distances.

Asleep or awake, I would keep my hand
>> on the small of your silken back
>> to turn the strange into the familiar.
You are the tiniest person I've held.
Deep inside me, I quiver like your chin
>> between cries. I lift you to my cheek, neck,
>> send thin, muscular signals into our brief caress:

Grow, shine, keep being. And be anything but maybe.
To the obscene headlines of August 1990
>> and to the armies of stunted persuasions
>> who would make their treacherous claims on you
I send arguments fierce and quick: No.

And to you, little boy: When you are
>> the weight of a man, do more than whimper
"I am only one, there is nothing I can do."

There is so much. &

Christmas Vigil of Mothers
At the Gates of the Pershing Missile Site, Mutlangen, Germany

On Christmas Eve they come with trees
To let the trees do vigil, tempt fate
In front of the alien gates. Barbed wire
Is the only decoration; the mothers' declaration—the trees.
The women plant them in the wire of thorns,
These mothers among their priests
And their tall crosses made of wood.
They step out of time and place,
Cradle their missing, their unforgettable children,
Hoping to fill the day with lullabies of silence.
Hoping the metallic trucks—with their loads of
Other people's missiles to be aimed at
Still other people's missiles only borders away—
Will not try to deliver themselves on Christmas.
Beyond the gates, enough confused mechanisms,
Enough already profaning the dead leaves and the scent of storm
And the bird cries gone off in search of trees not hung with
fear.
The mothers in their scarfs and cloth coats,
Their wearable placards,
Their values warm inside their ribs,
Will lay their peace in front of the gates.
There its echo will be an unassailable target
Until the missiles are taken away
And trees take their place
To speak in the falling stillness of snow
Of the glittering that will come to their arms
With the sun. ❧

Traveling

It's about borders.
Out there the land screams at its edges;
that is, people think it should.
So they send armies to shrink or bloat
what map makers have drawn
from the yankings of history.

On the borders they expect right
to stay on one side. But it thumps
and howls, skinning the sky
that never stops. It is borders
that suggest, give permission,
invite the yours and the mine
of the quarrels, separate, kill.

A border would divide even a piece of time
into here and hereafter.

But what a traveler finds
is that no one administrates
what flows between people.
Mortal connectedness, as if from enormous wings,
orders the comings, their passages,
the dissolution of borders in light
and the breath of human exchange.

Funny it took taking to the sky, then space
to obscure the detail, to let the traveler know
no matter how real, the borders don't exist:
They're only thinly dotted lines,
like the traveler, herself a small bundle of fibers
poised for passing when the soul
eradicates borders
and anywhere you go is going home. ॐ

War

6 : 4 5   A . M . ,   1 / 2 0 / 9 1

Where are we?
The world has gone out of my heart
        and taken it along.
Death flies sorties like fireworks over Baghdad
And mothers mask their children in Jerusalem
        for when it comes,
The underbelly of a new world order
Delivering no longer by hand.

At home we telephone each other
As each "too late" explodes
And what we pray for, like an ancient slogan,
Is undecipherable in the signals
        of jammed radar
        and targets on fire.

Mother, we always called you
Leaving or coming back
To say we were safe and unconfounded.
And Father, you were always there somewhere
Counting chances for a not impossible future.

How is it possible not to feel responsible
For the woman and her generations in the Bedouin tent
Or the pilot from North Carolina gone up in flames
        over the desert?

53

Not to curry the favor of sleep
       when only the connectedness of prayers
       can open the skies
       to drown the sirens
       and unclog the heart
       and re-chart the world
       screaming in the night?

Tomorrow I will fly my flag.
God, let it be for good. ❧

III.

Things Happen

Things Happen

I

Things happen. Early in the world you travel into them. One day
You rise without prayer in a far camp and silently hurry away.
Having slept under stars and still breathing the greyed fire,
Who would take time to suppose this the middle of a lifetime?

You whisper kisses to those left flowering, a big hand, a small foot
          uncovered.
You travel the sleepy gullies, come out of the mountains laughing:
Because it is morning and you and that son have places to go,
Even the heartless freeway is acceptable, having an end.
His traveling is dexterous, fast, like you used to ski,
You reading to him from the new owner's manual of how.

II

Things happen. A crash like a shot, your hand full of blood
From temple and eye, the split second. Speed ramming steel
Into your newly spent lifetime the blanks of bewildered abruption.
Not in on what was before you, gone the luxury of seeing, of choice.
From the highway, through the windshield the splatters of morning.
Smashed to floating that side of your face, what it held.

Instant the clouds, the passages saying You hear me?
Another place, a distant light, a flower in wind, you echoing Why?
Spilled questions wrenching your temple and eye to strenuous focus:
A dark navigable by caress and whisper. A stillness.

III

Things happen. As a writer you imagined yourself inside another,
Slowly connections emerging from disconnections. Now
Through pain you travel painlessly by a new Manual of How.
That son, a surgeon, turns hazard lights on, goes 90 to emergency.
"Impossible." Patrolmen, doctors, reporters heft the six-pound shaft.

To you nothing here is immediate, crucial, in the least attractive.

No expecting beyond hours of X-rays, stitches, shots, ice.

All that time returning, you vague about familiar hands,
Tangled in your head, the blow to trace, surely someone else's story.
Approaching landmarks like on a curve seeing where you've been,
Things happen by the light of a new Manual of How. ⁊⁊

When I Died

After the accident when I died
    I knew only about silences
and how to occupy them with
    travel and arrival I had nothing to say about.
Someone else lived in my skin
    not sorrowful, not curious
    not unglad, acknowledging no hunger
    no vocabulary of passions
    no calendar of things to come.
Only the pastels of having returned.

So if I now am at a distance
    and more and more
    connected to night
    and wake up with a closed smile
    that takes up my wrinkles

it is that I am occupied:
by the light that tells me
where I have been and will go and
listens with me in the ringing
and rejoicing of having had the time. ૏

You Heal

One morning you wake
and everything works
and almost nothing hurts.
After seven months
and the surgery up through
your mouth, screwed to metal plates
scars invisible, you even can focus.

After things happen
you heal. It takes its jagged course
upward and then
believe it or not,
so much for it,
and it is done
the chance of happening.

Then the heart of not
figuring a way back
just happens again
in the still world
like rain running the
skies and green becoming
the hand of the sun
with God standing by. &

Meditations on the Heavens

1. The Comet is an Angel Wing

Angel wings are on the beach
I found one shining in the sand
One late night looking for the comet
We'd been told would be near Pleiades

I found one shining in the sand
A nebulous and luminescent cloud like
We'd been told would be near Pleiades
A long curved vapor tail by the moon's first lifted lid

A nebulous and luminescent cloud now
Striated fragile rippled bone of wave tide wind
A long curved vapor tail by the moon's first lifted lid
The shell as smooth and rough as what we walk

Striated fragile rippled bone of wave tide wind
An ancient icon like the comet's head approaching sun
The shell as smooth and rough as what we walk
A celestial body grounded for our view

An ancient icon like a comet's head approaching sun
An angel wing was on the beach
A celestial body grounded for our view
One late night looking for the comet.

2. The Comet is a Darting Light

Suppose he really saw the vision, God, the angel
My church owns the story: Joseph in the grove, fourteen,
A supernatural sight of extraordinary beauty and significance
While praying for a truth that had eluded others

My church owns the story: Joseph in the grove, fourteen
Not unlike Joan, young Buddha, or Mohammed
While praying for a truth that had eluded others
From unusual encounter the gift more than surprising

Not unlike with Joan, young Buddha or Mohammed
It had to be believed, the unbelievable
In unusual encounter, the gift more than surprising.
Looking through binoculars the night I found the comet

It had to be believed, the unbelievable
The meteor, the incandescent sparkler writing names by Pleiades
Coming through binoculars the night I found the comet
More than white on black that no one else could see

The meteor, the incandescent sparkler writing names by Pleiades
Suppose he really saw the vision, God, the angel
More than white on black that no one else could see
A supernatural sight of extraordinary beauty and significance.

3. The Comet is Remembering

Not until today this small comet in my scalp:
The clattering of memory: the painting
In the chapel of my childhood against the organ loft:
Joseph kneeling at the elevated feet of the Father and the Son.

The clattering of memory, the painting,
Backdrop to the hymns, the bishop, and the sacrament,
Joseph kneeling at the elevated feet of the Father and the Son.
Did the artist put it in—the vision—or did I?

Backdrop to the hymns, the bishop, and the sacrament,
My quarter-century there, it rose indigenous as music.
Did the artist put it in—the vision—or did I?
In the Sacred Grove, sun streaming on the boy at prayer.

My quarter century there, it rose indigenous as music,
More real now than Palmyra, where I occupied one grown-up
        Sunday
The Sacred Grove: Sun streaming on the boy at prayer
Indelible on knowing, like features of a mother giving milk.

More real now than the Sacred Grove I occupied one grown-up
        Sunday
        Not until today this small comet in my scalp:
        Indelible on knowing, like the features of a mother giving milk:
        In the chapel of my childhood against the organ loft:
        the vision. ❧

63

Coming Up on Lake Powell

On the rising shimmer of green
I ski among the red cliffs.
Pressing into my one long foot I cling cut skim: solitary.
The jellied lake slices at my ankles, my heels slice back
and send against the rocks a diamond fan
twice the height of my slick hair.
My hands lock, then give. I fling the rope,
spread my hands on air and coast uncrucified
into the gulp of the water. Lying here on the cove,
head back, feet dangling, up to my ears in Lake Powell
I hear the lives I never lived.
My current one washes away in what is left of the boat.
On the skimpy distance, had by its motor,
it turns to circle back for me.
But 300 feet of water rock me, brashly amphibious,
eyes awake, ears wondering. Memory bobs
and finds its place:

> There on my eyelids is the frigid river hole
> that summer, and I no swimmer, hilarious,
> so long ago one of the five in the picture is dead.
> The other four with sixteen grown up children among us
> and only smiles the same.
> The midnight skinny dipping hoots across the lakes
> and separations, some quaint strains of that marine
> life clinging to the wet scalp of everything. ❧

Poet

A thought snaps,
a whole page deserves the torch.
The changing shape of a line
goes tumbling off a cliff.
Crash. Splat.
Do the world a favor, put it away.
Pretender! Spare yourself the frightful burden
of half knowing,
less than half saying. Who
are you trying to fool?
If you have anything to say it is
Here I am
no one in particular
and everyone.
Neatly nailed together
built to fly apart.
Burning under the glass
of my own eye. ❧

I am Delighted

I am delighted. My life goes well.
I must say it as clearly as I can
before I'm gone.
So little delight there can seem in the world.
Almost as if it's shameful or naive
to love what is there:

A new collapsible pair of glasses
flat in a one-inch pouch—imagine!
Can be worn inside my bra:
Anywhere the telephone book,
a needle, newsprint—it's OK.
Touch a key on my new computer,
Clean up window. And tiny icons
on a desk top scoot about for space—
alphabetical!
Take a 4 o'clock walk from Ketchum
past the fields and watch a young mare
and gelding frolicking like kittens,
a nine-year-old biker trying to look nonchalant
as he sails past you
with no hands.
Hear the brook getting in with
the white swans at the black pond.
Feel the sun making its last statement
to the fence posts.

Smell the perfume of the yellow haired
lady strolling with the short man's hand.
Nod as the Land Cruisers give way
to the languid redolence
of manure.
Back, find the word you've hunted for:
forage, jasmine, medallion.
Taste the strawberries on yogurt
at your own sink.
Let the shower have its way with
your hair.
Be tired.
After they have stood and sat and walked
and climbed the stairs, put those legs
to bed.
Talk not at all.
Take as long as you need
to find the fit.
And those eyes, let them close.
See, see, particles of delight
to sleep with
and be delightfully surprised by
tomorrow. ᐧ❦

The Tree Comes Down

Up our St. Mary's Drive yesterday they started
first with saws snarling among limbs
no doubt where nerve endings whine
and quiver.

A storm, I thought, first time
driving by the tree. One big wind
could bring it down. Likely sawed up
before it falls on someone. But rotten?
Mean spirited? We'd watched it grow.

Two hours later, I walked to it. Sawed
and split for being gathered up.
Sectioned on the ground it looks sweet
and sound throughout. Some error
by the surgeon. How much of sun and shower
dismantled in a morning and let down
out of itself a finger, a gold band at a time?

Anyhow, there it isn't, on the ground.
Maybe by spring, grass seed or baby crops sown
over the grave, lettuce, parsley, chives?
But by this evening what a confusion of shadows
and bewilderment of birds. ❧

Nurse Log

In the rain forest where the spiked hand
of lightning or stiff old age rattles a day
or night until stout trees no longer stand,
the Sitka spruce lies down to rich decay
and takes on another life. It will replace
itself five fold by offering a sapling fir
or spruce a straddling of its furrows twice
as sure as earth. It spreads the musky word
and cultivates its bed. Seed tells root. More
youngsters swing their leggy crotches and get
astride. These children, so enriched, can soar
on limbs and air their predecessors fed.
Sweet comfort for bequeather of the breath!
Far from sacrifice this giving life in death.* ✍

One to Get Ready

TO GRACE, AGE 10

Out of town, on a trip,
    I sat this morning in a white tub
        on the eighth floor of Chicago.
Unpossessed, I ran the steaming stream
    past reason, waited, ran some more,
        began to feel its watery undoing.
Stretched out full length, my shortness
    shorter than the tub (for once
        no need to worry that my hair
Was getting wet), I began to swell and float
    buoyant as a dolphin, rolling over
        even. How long since I had
Taken to a tub on breast and thigh, cheek
    down? I was a child in slippery
        frolic but slower, more
Deliberate in my convolutions, savoring
    the swish and loll. A plump euphoria
        reddened in my calves and toes, turned
My fingers into plums, then prunes. My opened
    eyes loved water not their own; hurrying
        seeped out of me like moisture from
A swimming suit hung unwrung out to dry.

Then—why? Some daring snickered in
the echo of my ear and I stood crazily
to face the shower giving me its
Head. Ablaze I reached and moved its plastic
knob to cold. It took its warm time
coming but then turned head-on
Into my seduced repose. Cool. Cooler. Colder.
Cold! Still ankle deep in draining hot
I took the needles in, starting at my
Scalp, the cold insistence on a rising. Gasping,
grinning, half surprised at being so alive, I
waited for the hot to go, the cold
Persuasions yipping at my wayward pulse three
stories down. How had I been so brave?
that now I stood, no water on at
All, tears of melted ice bristling on my
blazing skin like droplets in a skillet
saying It is time. &

Galloping Through Your Own Backyard

The pussy willow wears a yellow death mask.
It talks to the flames in the Japanese maple:

It says your mother isn't looking:
your father will not be crushed:

Those you love more than yourself
need not be terror hosting terror.

The orange eyes of the pyracantha
say Mount. Ride. The back, the saddle

can rise here too all sweaty and sweet.
The newly shod hooves can clamor the leaves

and throng the cement, make it sound less grief stricken.
But they are only the first exposures.

You can ride off on the wooden steps
down over across as if on the covered bridge.

Here, hold the leather, the rein on the lip, the jaw
working, the huge frame pounding between your knees,

collected, as surefooted in this fenced clearing as in the deep
woods where the wind never reaches the ground.

There, gallop at the bottom. Circle tighter and tighter
on the leaves given to grass, withers and rump sleek

and connected, head high as hearkening ears.
You can speak that language learned only in solitude.

It comes back like the black roots of your grey hair,
showing, the last settlement coming to life. ❧

Nirvana

Twenty-two days alone have done it:
nights and mornings blending like fog and sky.
Sometimes it takes that to learn how it is
when you get to wake up one nerve at a time:

First you prepare for sleep   tired but not too.
And slowly: ablutions nothing
in the gentle eruptions in your head:
a line from a poem   a place in a story   a collecting
of ideas who have yet to meet: the face
of your grandmother   the hand of your love
your child at different ages   your sense of forever.

You are ready for bed without knowing
everything in for speculation. Formalities
take shape: kneeling   sitting   lowering to a pillow
nothing yet touching off edges and ends
trying to let go of themselves:

Perhaps you will read them to rest.
You will know when it is time:
You will reach for the light
barely sink from it to remember your scalp:
how it likes to draw back on its goods
free its face to feel: the pillow   the cheek
the temple   the jaw   the ear   flush with the down
the case . . .

That is all.

Then it is morning   probably not late:
No sound has found you   only dreams
not wanting to be lost. An eye might flicker
toward the window   for a time:
No matter. The lid is unwilling
to part for long with what is behind it:
the generous granter of wisps waiting for form
liberators, informants
characters of a language never inconceivable.

You cohabit the space that is nowhere:
Drafts and injections   spill within you:
You are empty and full   by now weightless.
Enjoy the luxury of levitation: Nothing
is separate: No wrist or hip   has ligament   muscle.

Examine the comfort of everything
come into place: tongue to mouth   palate   teeth
surfaces having found each other:
legs   sheets   bottom   the outside of
your ribs   arms   shoulder   what they lie on.

Your feet are conscious of their soles
your eyes aware of being covered   affronted if not:
Adopt the covering   the remaining:
your heart containing itself going nowhere
then ticking to attention in your palms.

Breathing exists on its own: a bellows on automatic
slow   deep. It is not yet time for a thought:
Acquainting is still elsewhere:
Impressions come like invisible ink
by formulas that refuse formulation:
Your outer boundaries sift into everywhere.
You are taken. As if giving in to great weariness
you are rested awake: This is the home of the Muse:
of the Holiest of Ghosts. You wait here longer
accepting   honoring. Until:
you are given the time to return:

Gravity and willingness having looked out for you.
Resistance must come as the gentle inflating
of a balloon: one breath at a time.
You pay attention: Under the soft ringing
you can hear your heart   first in your ears
then in your throat   finally in itself
rhythmic   delicate   sound   promising:

Gradually your light moves outside of you.
Dimly then you admit sounds: stirrings
of systems inside   out: viscera   brain
furnace   plumbing   a breeze   a bird.
Fingers   toes   start to work themselves.
Slowly joints unflop. You acquiesce: fold like a rag doll
out of yourself   strung only to where you have been:

76

Your neck is your pulley: up   out.
You take shape:
You blink at what has been waiting
and step toward the day in peace
prepared: by what passes understanding.

You will save this morning   for protection
against days when you will be jarred awake:
not knowing who has been   to visit in the night. ৯

Speak of Reverence for Being

"Hi, this is David," your answering machine said again,
your voice rich as when you were in radio.
"I can't answer the phone right now,
but leave your message, and I'll get back to you
as soon as I can." I knew you were dead.

The AIDS that killed Paul there in Chicago
had swept you away too.
No more rivers to pilot,
Haitian children to take toys to,
gospel sing-a-longs to lead. No more loneliness.
"No, they don't come now. When you've seen
so many friends die, you can't stand to be in on one more."

Why couldn't there have been a Paul for you?
There. Constant. Attending to your thirst,
finding help for your pain.
Five years almost to the day
since your voice called to say, "He's gone, he's well."
Paul, my psychic painter friend,
who knew like you about worship.
You were 35, he not quite. Your mothers, 52, both.
Your best day when you let each other meet,
mothers, fathers, sons beloved, attentive to the end.
What blood must I let to tell my sunny world
the aching bleakness of my tears? ❧

Love Song at the End of Summer

It is clear now, body. Every day can be late August,
after the birth of babies, never quite cold.

But one must learn early what you are for forever.

Good old leather tiger, half domesticated
by paws in pans and shoulders hung too often with beaded fur,
you may think I forget. But you do not let me.
By now I know better. I come back.

Still, you never take me not surprised, faithful one,
by how to arrive, and the pleasure of sweat,
and how to shiver away the bee.
You move to the song behind the dance.
Even after a standard, plain white, unstriped day,
you ripple in our sleep and wait, mostly unperplexed.

And when, no matter how faint, the music breathes
behind the catcalls of too much to do, you muster
almost without my inclining, potent as needing to dance,
to pace off the house, the garden of weeds, the clogged creek,
and the midnight clutch of vagrancies. You pad from
some spring, and wild, except for my importuning,
go. To do it all.

When we lie down, it will be like the squirrel there,
unflagging in the last swift moving in the leaves,
August stashed in crisp piles above the dust.

I may find no way at all without your sleek taking.

Under the wrinkles that tell you no, I can hear you now
saying, "I still love you," and to time, "Leave her alone." ❧